Letter to a Jewish Friend

LETTER TO A JEWISH FRIEND

The simple and extraordinary story of
Pope John Paul II and his Jewish school friend

Gian Franco Svidercoschi

Translated by Gregory Dowling

Crossroad · New York

1994

The Crossroad Publishing Company
370 Lexington Avenue, New York, NY 10017

Copyright © 1993 by Arnoldo Mondadori
The right of Gian Franco Svidercoschi to be identified as the Author of
the Work has been asserted by him in accordance with the Copyright,
Designs and Patents Act 1988.

New material included in the American edition Copyright © 1994 by the
Anti-Defamation League.

Originally published by Arnoldo Mondadori Editore as *lettera a un
amico ebreo: La storia semplice e straordinaria dell'amico ebreo di
Karol Wojtyla*, 1993.

First English language edition published by Hodder & Stoughton,
London, England, 1994.

Printed in the United States of America

Library of Congress Catalogue Card Number: 94-69812

ISBN: 0-8245-1482-3

Prologue:
Letters to our Readers

Letter from John Cardinal O'Connor

This haunting, poignant story of the extraordinary and beautiful friendship between Jerzy Kluger and Karol Wojtyla, a friendship deepened, not lessened, by Karol Wojtyla's becoming Pope John Paul II, is itself a paradigm of the Anti-Defamation League's relationship with the Catholic Church. While the ADL consistently opposes defamation, it is equally committed to the advance of understanding.

The conversations between Jerzy and Karol in their student days reveal what I profoundly believe to be the "naturalness" of what relations between every Jew and every Catholic *should* be. Unstrained, they have a taken-for-granted quality about them which I personally find in my own relationships with Jewish friends in New York and elsewhere, as when a Rabbi friend asks me to pray for his sick son. Indeed, without wanting to be pretentious, I must confess that the conversations remind me very much of my own televised conversation with Elie Wiesel.

I can not but believe that both in his student days and in his current life as Pope, Karol Wojtyla, now John Paul II, was and is unselfconsciously shaped by his fundamental gratitude for Judaism as the very root of his Catholicism. I suspect that such accounts in part, at least, for his genuine surprise when any of his words or actions or omissions offend our Jewish brothers and sisters. He seems simply to assume that his love for them and for Judaism itself is so strong that his good intentions should be recognized, even if what he says or does or fails to say or do might be negatively construed.

Jerzy, himself, seems to believe such of his old friend, for he resolves to renew the long-ago schoolboy relationship even though now Karol is Pope, and some of Jerzy's friends question the relationship. I would like to meet Jerzy. He reminds me of some of my friends in the ADL and a variety of other Jewish organizations. I puzzle them at times, they disagree with me on certain issues, but they break bread with me shamelessly, advise me forthrightly, and forgive me the otherwise unforgivable because they know that I love them.

Not long ago I saw a beautiful television show based on correspondence between George Bernard Shaw and a Benedictine Abbess. It was exquisitely done. I would hope that one day soon the ADL would translate Gian Franco Svidercoschi's *Letter to a Jewish Friend* into the magic of television, to touch the hearts of millions of Jews and Christians even more impellingly, if possible, than he does in his book. But whether they do so or not, in this publication alone, readers are given a precious gift.

JOHN CARDINAL O'CONNOR
Archbishop of New York

Letter from Abraham H. Foxman

The story told in this book, *Letter to a Jewish Friend*, by Gian Franco Svidercoschi about two childhood friends, both Polish—one a Catholic and the other a Jew—is a simple story, but also an extraordinary one. A story about friendship that crosses all religious and social boundaries should, in fact, be entirely normal and commonplace. Unfortunately, however, this has not always been the case—not in present times and certainly not in the past. That is why this book is so special and important—with its description of the strength and beauty of a friendship and the contribution it makes, through the example it sets, to the creation of a better world in which every human being may enjoy the respect he or she deserves.

The very special significance of this book also lies in the historical events providing the backdrop for the story: the Holocaust, which cancelled from the face of the earth one third of the Jewish people; the terrible world war in which hundreds of thousands of Poles perished, amidst countless other victims; the chaos that then descended upon Europe and the rest of the world.

But the most extraordinary aspect of the true story told in this book is the fact that the Catholic friend eventually rose in the hierarchy of the church, becoming, first, a high official and, ultimately, a Pope, adopting the name of John Paul II. Meanwhile, in the same post-war period, the Jewish friend also comes to live in Rome, and here the two renew their old friendship.

This story in itself has the power of dissipating the stereotypes and prejudices that still provide obstacles to human relations, especially those between the Jewish and Christian communities of the world. It was therefore natural that The Anti-Defamation League—founded to combat anti-Semitism, prejudice and discrimination, with the aim of creating a better society based on mutual respect—would see in this book an important contribution towards the achievement of its ideals.

Pope John Paul II's deep commitment to the great rapprochement between the Catholic Church and the Jewish people has been fundamental, and one of its crowning achievements has been the establishment of full diplomatic relations between the Holy See and the State of Israel. Israel and the Jews of the diaspora have been moved by John Paul II's many, heart-felt references to the sin of anti-Semitism exemplified in the horror of the Holocaust. May the new relations between Israel and the Vatican, between the church and the Jewish people, help us and the rest of the world to move a step closer to "Shalom."

ABRAHAM H. FOXMAN
National Director
Anti-Defamation League

Letter from Edward Cardinal Cassidy

Gian Franco Svidercoschi's decision to publish the story of the friendship between Karol Wojtyla and Jerzy Kluger is one that will bring joy and tears to those who read his account. For it is not only the story of a life-long friendship between two neighbours of Wadowice in Poland, one of whom we know as Pope John Paul II, but it brings the reader into close and intimate touch with the horrors of the Shoah, or so-called Holocaust.

For this friend of Pope John Paul II, Jerzy Kluger, comes from what was a relatively large Jewish population of Wadowice, almost entirely wiped out by the Nazi persecution during the Second World War.

This moving account of the relationship between the young Karol Wojtyla and his Jewish friend throws a special light on Pope John Paul's dedication to the promotion of Catholic-Jewish relations. There is no doubt that under the present Pontificate those relations have improved greatly. There is a new spirit of mutual understanding and respect, of good-will and reconciliation, of cooperation and common goals between Jews and Catholics, and much of the credit for this goes to the Pope who not only has opened the doors of the Vatican to Jewish leaders coming to Rome, but has visited them on his pastoral journeys throughout the world and taken every possible occasion to address in his speeches questions of concern to the two faith communities. It is this Pope who for the first time visited the Great Synagogue of Rome and presided over a special Concert in the Vatican in commemoration of the Holocaust.

There are two phrases in *Letter to a Jewish Friend* which help us to understand this special attention on the part of Pope John

Paul II to Catholic-Jewish relations. The first is the response made by the young Wojtyla to Jerzy Kluger when the latter sought him out in the Parish Church of Wadowice in order to tell him that he has passed the examination for admission to high school. A lady parishioner was surprised to see this young son of the chairman of the Jewish community of Wadowice in a Catholic Church. But the young Karol, or Lolek as he was affectionately known to his friends, burst out laughing when Jerzy mentioned this. "Why?" he asked. "Aren't we all God's children?"

The other episode comes much later in life, when Wojtyla is in Rome for the final session of the Second Vatican Council as Archbishop of Cracow. Jerzy is also in Rome, residing far from his native land, unable to be reconciled with the loss of his mother and sister in the Nazi extermination camp of Auschwitz and the destruction of all that was the Jewish presence in Wadowice. They meet, they walk, they talk. There is great emotion and much sadness in that meeting. At the end they embrace and Jerzy hears words from the Archbishop that he was not expecting: "One day, all Jews and Christians will be able to meet in this fashion."

It is to make these words a reality that Pope John Paul II has dedicated so much of his time and thought over the past fifteen years. I have had the privilege for five of these years of being closely associated with His Holiness in this task. Reading Svidercoschi's book helps me to understand the special approach to this relationship that guides the work, under the present Holy Father, of the Holy See's Commission for Religious Relations with the Jews.

A final word is addressed to anyone who doubts about the reality of the Shoah or Holocaust. Read this short but moving story of the friendship of Karol Wojtyla to Jerzy Kluger. I don't believe that you will be able to doubt any longer.

EDWARD CARDINAL CASSIDY
President
Pontifical Commission for
Religious Relations with the Jews

Letter from Rabbi Leon Klenicki

Letter to a Jewish Friend is the story of two friends, an epic of mutual understanding across Europe. It is the saga of two men born in Poland who shared family events as well as the political problems of their country, military dictatorship, and anti-Semitism.

This is the story of Karol Wojtyla–Pope John Paul II–and Jerzy Kluger, his Jewish friend who has lived in Rome since 1945. Both are from Wadowice, a city sixty kilometers from Cracow, and have known each other since childhood. Wadowice was a city of 10,000 people, of which 2,000 were Jewish. But nothing is left of the Jewish community save the synagogue building, rebuilt under the inspiration of Pope John Paul II, and the Jewish cemetery.

Pope John Paul II is deeply concerned about the ever-present sin of anti-Semitism. Recently, he called the attention of the European Bishops to the scourge of racism. In his speech to forty European Bishops attending a meeting in the Hole See, June 5-7, 1990, to prepare the 1991 Special Assembly of European Synod of Bishops, representing both Eastern and Western Bishops, Pope John Paul II said:

> The war itself with its immense cruelty, a cruelty that reached its most brutal expression in the organized extermination of the Jews, as well as of the Gypsies and of other categories of people, revealed to the European the other side of a civilization that he was inclined to consider superior to all others. Certainly, the war also brought out people's readiness to show solidarity and make heroic sacrifices for a just cause. But these admirable aspects of the war experience seemed to be overwhelmed by the immensity of evil and destruction, not only on the material plane, but also in

the moral order. Perhaps in no other war in history has man been so thoroughly trampled upon in his dignity and fundamental rights. An echo of the humiliation and even desperation caused by such an experience could be heard in the question often repeated after the war: How can we go on living after Auschwitz? Sometimes another question presented itself: Is it still possible to speak about God after Auschwitz?

Karol and Jerzy were separated by the Second World War. Karol went underground fighting the Nazis, and Jerzy fled through Russia to join the Polish army in North Africa and Italy. They met again after the war and continued their childhood relationship. Karol was already a priest and became later the Archbishop of Cracow. Their friendship continued to our own day in friendly conversations, sharing food and thought.

The brotherly relationship of Lolek-John Paul II and Jurek-Jerzy Kluger is a symbol that makes possible the reality of peace and friendship. It is a symbol that proclaims the possibility of Catholics and Jews together witnessing God, respectful of each other and their differences. Their friendship is a relationship in God, towards God. A French Jewish philosopher, Emmanuel Levinas, whom the Pope respects much, has described the possibilities of such a friendship in words that are a message to all of us. He says:

> The existence of God is sacred history itself, the sacredness of man's relation to man through which God may pass.

This is a message that John Paul II and Jerzy Kluger are sharing with us. It is a guide to all of us, a call to friendship and mutual recognition, of respectful acceptance of the other as a person of faith, dominated by affection and the call of God.

May this reality, the encounter of Catholics and Jews, open the doors to God, allowing the Eternal to be a reality in our everyday life and the life of the community.

RABBI LEON KLENICKI
Director
Department of Interfaith Affairs
Anti-Defamation League

Letter to a Jewish Friend

CHAPTER ONE

Jerzy starts the story from the end. And he recounts it quickly, as if he were afraid of forgetting something.

"I didn't want to go, to Poland I mean. After all that time, and everything that had happened, I didn't feel like going back."

They were expecting him in Wadowice, the small town sixty or so kilometres from Cracow where he had lived until the age of twenty. They wanted him to be present at the unveiling of a plaque on the site where the synagogue had once stood.

The Nazis had blown it up one foggy morning in November 1939. They had forced a group of civilians to watch the explosion. Frightened old men, poor women dressed in black.

"That'll show the Poles the way to treat these filthy Jews!" the SS Captain had yelled before giving the order for the fuse to be ignited.

When this happened, Jerzy had already set off eastwards with his father. He heard about it much later.

He heard what had become of the inhabitants of the ghetto, his own family, his friends.

This was why he had no wish to go back. He was afraid that the same thing might happen to him as had happened to his cousin: he had visited Poland, returned to the United States and, four weeks later, had suddenly died; the emotional strain had been too much for his heart.

Jerzy was afraid of having to relive certain memories: not happy recollections of youth, but anguished memories he had borne with him for years. He knew he would not even be able to enter his old house. They had told him that the front door was closed, nailed up, the interior full of rubble. And that the park, a gift from his grandfather to the city, was now in ruins.

"My sister and I always used to go there as children to play."

No, he had no wish to go back. The weight of his past, as a Pole and a Jew, was too much.

"Two peoples fed by the same suffering," Slonimski had written. "The two saddest peoples on this earth."

Thus Jerzy had turned the invitation down. He would not go.

But then that letter arrived, one spring afternoon in 1989. At first he could not believe it. A letter with the Papal seal addressed to him: "Distinguished Engineer Jerzy Kluger." It was written by his old school-mate, Karol Wojtyla, and signed, John Paul II.

"Dear Jurek . . ."

The letter reminded him – as if to urge him to go – that on May 9th a plaque would be unveiled in memory of the Jews exterminated by the Nazis.

"Many of these fellow countrymen and coreligionists of yours, who were killed, were companions of ours at the primary school and then the high-school in Wadowice, where we took our school-leaving exams together fifty years ago . . . I well remember the synagogue, which was close to our school. I can still see the long lines of the faithful, who made their way to the synagogue on feast days to pray . . ."

At this point, Jerzy laid aside all his previous doubts and uncertainties. He took his decision. He went back to Poland, to Wadowice, after fifty years. And he did what Karol had suggested ("if it strikes you as appropriate"): in front of the plaque he read aloud the letter he had been sent. Thus he, a Jew, represented his friend the Pope.

Then, when it was all over, he thought he could not just go off again. It would be cowardly.

"I must at least see the high-school," he told himself.

And he made his way to the institute, named after Marcin Wadowita, in Mickiewicz Street. He gazed at the door, the walls, the inscription with two lines from Tibullus: ". . . *Et manibus puris sumite fontis aquam*", and his eight years of high school unreeled before him like a film.

He thus plucked up courage, and continued walking.

7

It was lunchtime now. There was nobody on the streets. He felt as if his heart were bursting. Familiar voices sounded in his ears. But his memories were confused.

"Now who used to live there?"

Finally, to his surprise, he found himself in the main square, his square, the Rynek.

He had often wondered how he would feel at such a moment. And now he just felt nothing. It was as if the sun were in his eyes. He couldn't see a single thing, and he couldn't understand a single thing. It all seemed just the same as ever and, at the same time, utterly different, changed. The fountain. The withered trees. The hardware shop. The newspaper stand. Balamut, the motorbike and pushbike man. The chemist's. The stalls of the weekly market that were just then being dismantled.

But gradually he managed to get his bearings. There on the right, next to the parish church, was his primary school in the Town Council building. On the left, his father's office. Once there had been a name-plate outside: "Lawyer Dr Wilhelm Kluger." A man who was forever dropping Latin proverbs between one cigarette and another. He was a famous lawyer, much esteemed and respected, and the chairman of the Jewish community. Wadowice, before the Second World War, had 10,000 inhabitants, 2,000 of whom were Jews.

Jerzy lingered on, exploring the square. Over there on the far side was where he had lived: on the first floor of a building with large rectangular windows that stood on the corner of Zatorska Street. It felt remote, alien. The Nazis had turned it into the Gestapo headquarters, then the communists had requisitioned it. He could not even look at it. It was as if they had profaned it. And along with his house, his family. The women in his family.

The women! His mother, Rozalia, beautiful and gentle, but also extremely energetic. It was she who ran the house, who took charge of the administration, not the lawyer. She was always so full of life. A wonderful dancer and skater. The only thing that ever gave her any problems was the piano. Her husband had set up a musical quartet with some friends, and they rehearsed in the living room. Rozalia accompanied them on the piano, but they always ended up quarrelling.

And his sister, a few years younger than him: Stefania, always called Tesia. Blonde, with blue eyes and a cheerful disposition. She was a tennis champion. At school she always got top marks. She never did anything that might irritate her parents: the complete opposite of her brother, who was somewhat unruly, a rebel.

And Grandmother Huppert, on his mother's side. She often went out for walks with the parish priest, Canon Prochownik; as she got older, she spent her days in an armchair, by the window that looked out onto the Rynek. It was as if she had her own "secret service", she always knew immediately what her grandson was up to.

"Remember, only remember."

Jerzy always repeated this to himself. Remembering was the only way to survive. To honour the dead, but also to continue to live.

And above all he remembered those Friday evenings, when the Jewish sabbath began. The dining-room, which was heated in the winter by the large ceramic stove, was only dimly lit. His mother, standing by a candelabrum, would light four candles one after the other. And so, slowly, the room would come to flickering life. The others would be sitting round the table, Jerzy and his father with their heads covered, Grandmother Huppert and Tesia. His mother would hold her hands out over the candles; then she would raise them, with the fingers still spread out, to her eyes. And in a low voice she would say the benediction.

"Blessed are You, O lord our God, King of the Universe, who have sanctified us with your precepts, and have commanded us to kindle the light in honour of the Sabbath."

As he stood in the square in Wadowice, Jerzy felt something melt inside himself. There was no longer a knot in his belly. His tension was slackening. And he started to cry, but without despair. Subduedly. Gently. As if it were an act of liberation.

And for the first time he looked at his house. And he went back down the path of those distant years. Those happy years.

CHAPTER TWO

Every morning they would meet at the entrance to the primary school. They were two thin children, with short-cropped hair.

"Hello, Jurek."

"Hello, Lolek."

They always used these friendly diminutives: "Georgie" and "Charlie". They were great friends. They had a good many friends. Some in their class, like the Piotrowski twins, known as "the-laughing-ones".

In the summer they played in the Skawa, the stream that ran through Wadowice. The water was shallow and cold, but you could swim in it all the same. In winter they met at the Venice Bar, where the tennis-court was frozen over and used as a skating rink; in the evening they turned the lights on and played a gramophone; there was a cheerful atmosphere. Or they would go to some pond, which had been transformed into a sheet of ice, and play hockey with rudimentary sticks. On one occasion the arch of Lolek's eye got split open by a carelessly wielded stick; blood streamed down his face, terrifying everybody.

When they were about ten, they started to go on major "expeditions". They ventured as far as Lysa Gora, two miles away, where there was a good ski slope. Or to Leskowiec, at an altitude of almost a thousand metres, although it took half a day to walk there, and there was the risk of running into wolves. Or they might choose Grandmother Huppert's farm, her beautiful garden with big apple-trees and cherry-trees. Once, after gorging on cherries, they came back with terrible stomach-aches.

Lolek was quite capable of getting up in the middle of a game and saying: "Now it's time to study."

Jurek often went and did his homework at his friend's house, in Koscielna Street, behind the parish church. A modest but dignified house that intrigued him. A masculine house, unlike his own, dominated by women.

Lolek had lost a sister before he was even born. And in 1929 his mother, Emilia, died, while still young. He never talked of her. He only remembered that when he was small, she had taught him to make the sign of the cross. He had a photo of her by his bed. A beautiful lady, slightly built, with a gentle but lively expression; however, her health was delicate, she was always being treated by the doctors; she had to take things easy, so Lolek was often kept away from her.

His father was not the remarrying sort. He was very much in love with his wife. And having retired – he had been a regular officer in the administrative services of the Austrian and then Polish army – he had decided to devote himself completely to his younger son. The other one, Edmund, was a doctor in Bielsko (he too was to die prematurely from scarlet fever). Lolek always remembered going, at the age of ten, to the legendary Jagellonic University in Cracow for his brother's degree ceremony.

And so it was the Captain, as he was known to everyone, who looked after Lolek and the house. Both a father and a mother. They would have lunch at the Banas canteen in the same street. But it was he who prepared breakfast and dinner, washed the dishes, and did the cleaning. As a young man he had learnt tailoring, so it was no problem for him to adapt old uniforms and make a suit for his son. But he was also a scholar and did research into Polish history.

He had grizzled hair and a moustache. His expression seemed severe, but he was actually gentle and courteous in his manners. He had a great sense of duty. And while he demanded a lot from himself, he had no need to do so from his son.

He taught Lolek to swim, to study, to live. And he taught him to pray, to contemplate the mystery of God. When Lolek got up early, he would often find his father on his knees praying. A scene that remained impressed on his eyes and in his heart.

Jurek would go running up the steep staircase that led to the first floor, the Wojtylas' flat. There was a kitchen, and in the hall a majolica bowl for holy water, as in church. Then the two rooms of the house: the bedroom where they slept together, with the Captain's sabre hanging on the wall, and a little altar to one side; and the living room, where father and son would sometimes play football with a ball made of rags. One of the three windows, the brightest, gave on to the southern wall of the parish church, which had a sun-dial with the words: *"Tempus fugit, aeternitas manet"*. The passing of time in the house was marked by the sound of church-bells.

When his friend arrived, Lolek would clear his desk, putting away his collection of toy soldiers. Then he would pull out his books, and they would start their revision. A few poems to learn by heart. Some dates from history.

"When was the first invasion of Poland?"

"In 1241, by the Tartars."

"And when was the Swedish invasion checked?"

"On December 26th, 1655, at Czestochowa."

"And how many partitions . . ."

Without fail, as soon as they let out their first yawns, the Captain would appear.

"So what are you doing? Tired already?"

He would go and get a book of old illustrations. The heroic days of Poland. The uprising against the Russians.

The repression. The number of people forced into exile: Mickiewicz, Slowacki, Chopin . . .

Lolek and Jurek would kneel on their chairs to get a better view. It was fascinating, stirring. They would kneel there and listen with their mouths and eyes wide open. Like that time when the Captain started to read a poem by Cyprian Norwid dedicated to Chopin:

". . . from one alley to the next/Caucasian horses burst forth/Like swallows before the storm/Darting in front of the regiments/Hundreds and hundreds/A building set ablaze, then extinguished/Then in flames once again, and there/Against the wall/I see the foreheads of the widows in mourning/Driven by the rifle-butts/And although blinded by smoke I see again,/Along the colonnade/Like a coffin on shoulders/Your piano being carried . . . falling . . . falling! . . ."

It was a story that gripped them, the soldiers, the horses, the war, although they did not understand all of it. Then the Captain would close the book with a smile.

"Don't worry. When you are older you will understand the history of your country better."

It was the tacit signal that the lesson was over. A quick goodbye, and then down the stairs, two at a time, to join their friends. But at the bottom, in the dim courtyard, they had to slow down. Mrs Szczepanska would be staring at them disapprovingly. She lived on the ground floor and, when Lolek's mother died, she had looked after him. She had been Mrs Kluger's school-companion, now she was Tesia's school-teacher. Jurek already knew what she would say.

"Did you study at all? You don't want to be shown up by your sister, do you?"

Another scolding, to add to those that he got daily from Grandmother Huppert.

"Why don't you study like Lolek?"

But Jurek did study. And he proved it. He could not contain his joy that rainy afternoon at the end of June, when it was confirmed that they had all passed the entrance exam to the high-school. So he too had made it into the "big" school, the one that was called "Super Universitas Vadoviensis".

He went out into the Rynek and made his way straight to church. He saw Lolek at the altar dressed in an altar-boy's white surplice. He wanted to tell him about it in a low voice, but in fact everyone heard him.

"Lolek, Lolek, you've passed!"

A stern glance from his friend silenced him. He stood to one side and waited until the end.

A woman passed by and looked at him in surprise.

"Aren't you the son of the chairman of the Jewish community?" and she went off without even waiting for an answer. Jurek wouldn't have known what to answer in any case.

Lolek came up to him.

"What did she want?"

"I don't know. Maybe she was surprised to see a Jew in church."

Lolek burst out laughing. "Why? Aren't we all God's children?"

Jurek was glad to hear him say so. And he was even happier at the way he had said it.

CHAPTER THREE

"The best years of my life," says Jurek.

Suddenly his eyes light up. He stares ahead of himself, his eyes focused on nothing, as if to concentrate, to remember things better. Those eight years at the high-school, from 1930 to 1938, were years of study and hard work. But they were also carefree years, full of fun. And above all it was a time of friendship. He had had so many friends. And it is their faces, rather than words, that now flood back into his mind. Clearly. Distinctly. They bring with them all the sensations and emotions of that wonderful, unrepeatable period of his life. When youth was a heady perfume. And Wadowice was a small haven of peace. And it looked as if Poland would remain untouched by the stormclouds massing over Europe.

Wyspianski sang in one of his plays: "Let war break out all over the world/So long as the Polish countryside remains quiet/So long as the Polish countryside remains peaceful."

There were about forty pupils in Jurek's class. They

had all changed a little since their very first days at the high-school. They were more self-confident. Their faces were more adult. Their hair was longer, often combed back. Lolek had a thick mass of hair that just wouldn't stay in place. Maybe because he always came running into school, at the very last moment.

Stanislaw Banas was the richest boy in the class. His parents had one of the six cars in Wadowice and a stable with 200 horses; in spring the children came to school in a splendid carriage. But Stanislaw never gave himself airs, he was friendly with everyone.

Teofil Bojes was the poorest; his father was a miner. He was very intelligent. And he always made it his business to smooth over quarrels between his companions, to get them to behave better.

There were the politically committed ones, like Zdzislaw Bernas, with socialist ideas; he lived in a nearby village and commuted. And Rudolf Kogler, the "Marshal", who acted as the students' representative with the school authorities; in the afternoon he was in charge of the library, where they read, played ping-pong or – in secret – "Ferbel", a kind of Austrian poker.

There were the sporting types, like Wiktor Kesek and Zbigniew Silkowski, the station-master's son. Zbigniew was Wojtyla's desk-companion. At first he was an agnostic, and took little interest in religion; but then, under his friend's influence, he moved towards the

Church and joined the Society of Mary of which Lolek was the chairman.

And there was Tadeusz Czuprynski, tall, elegant, the "Don Giovanni" of the school. His mother, to restrain his exuberance, had sent him to a private school run by the Pallottine Fathers; but he had escaped, breaking his leg in his flight; nonetheless he had managed to go back to his old high-school.

Two of the more studious boys were Tomasz Romanski and Jan Kus. Jan was very good at helping his companions. He was very skilful at whispering answers and slipping notes, without ever being found out.

There were the Piotrowski twins who had invented the "Pleasure-Seekers' Club", maybe by way of answer to the "Abstinents' Circle" (who did not smoke or drink); and was founded by Lolek.

There was Zdzislaw Przybyla, who drew caricatures of his teachers and companions.

And there were two other Jewish boys, apart from Kluger: Zygmunt Selinger, who was exceptionally strong; he used to help his father to load sacks of flour; and Leopold Zweig, always having to repeat his exams, a great smoker, a great womaniser and above all a truly great football player, the best in Wadowice.

But there were also two anti-semitic students. One, short and stocky, was only any good at fighting. But the other had a subtle mind, and was always prepared to take people on in a dialectical confrontation. His key argument was "Jewish communism": he accused the Jews of being the main force behind the Bolshevik revolution.

And in addition to the disputes at school, there were heated football matches. To form teams more quickly, they would split up into Catholics and Jews, who would be joined by friends from other classes. The respective goal-keepers were Lolek, nicknamed "Martyna" after a famous player, and Poldek Goldberger, the dentist's son, the size of a wardrobe. The goal-posts were formed by jackets and satchels.

They would always begin with noble promises on both sides. Then, at the first chance, they would give way to brazenly intentional fouls, shin-hacking, spitting and insults.

"Get the Jew!"

And so, systematically, the disputants had to be separated, tempers had to be cooled.

But these were just episodes. It was certainly not part of daily life, at least not until the sixth year of high-school. Life in the classroom, all things considered, was generally pleasant. The schoolmasters were strict, but taught well. And, in some ways, they were amusing.

Panczakiewicz, the gymnastics teacher, organised sporting challenges with other schools, almost small-scale Olympics.

Klimczyk, the Polish teacher, known as "Maszynista",

the engine-driver, used to take the students to the theatre in Cracow to listen to the great Juliusz Osterwa.

Heriadin (natural science) would apologise profusely whenever he had to give a bad mark, and he used to leave his cigarettes on the desk. They were regularly pinched by the students to smoke in the toilets during the breaks.

Greek was taught by two different teachers in succession. First the much-feared Damasiewicz. Small, ugly, but always highly elegant, with gleaming shoes. The moment he entered the class he could tell if anyone had been smoking.

"You're a bunch of stinking scoundrels!"

He would start to question them. If nobody could answer, he would invariably finish with Lolek. And he addressed him strangely, cutting his surname in half: something that in Polish sounded like "Tela".

"Don't even *you* know, Tela?"

And he would fly into a temper if he heard so much as a giggle.

"Just what is there inside those stupid heads of yours? I'll bet there isn't even straw!"

He noticed Lolek. "Just look. Even Tela's laughing! What is the matter with you?"

One afternoon Jurek went to the cinema, with a friend and two young hairdressers, even though it was against the rules for students. They could only go if the school authorities put up an official notice, granting permission.

Suddenly the film-reel broke, the lights went on in the cinema, and Kluger found Damasiewicz just a few seats away. The teacher turned scarlet with rage.

"Out! Straight home!"

He gave him a bad conduct mark. Not content with that, he called his father and told him the whole story. . As a punishment, Jurek missed out on the whole skiing season.

Then Szeliski came along. He was nicknamed "Krupa", which was the name of an extremely unappetising barley soup. And they played sadistic jokes on him, such as nailing his galoshes to the floor or putting glue down his coatsleeves. Even Lolek, who was always more reluctant, would agree to do impersonations of him. But "Krupa" was a good sort. He never got angry.

Someone who did get angry was Gebhardt, the history teacher. Tall, serious, cold, a typical intellectual. He had socialist leanings and used to wear a red tie on the first of May.

The students had to wear a dark blue uniform, even outside the school, with the number 374, the school's emblem, clearly displayed. Unless accompanied by their parents, they were not supposed to leave their homes after eight p.m. (in winter) or nine (in summer). These were old rules that had remained in force from the Austrian days. And, since they were anachronistic, they were not always respected. Some of the teachers themselves interpreted them elastically. But others were not so accommodating. Out of respect for tradition they remained strict, inflexible.

If Gebhardt caught a boy, he was in for trouble. What was worse, he would often go to the park with his dog, a brown setter, and make his way through the trees and bushes of the "Avenue of Love" to surprise the couples.

Nothing serious ever went on. Just an innocent hug or kiss. Indeed, the only serious thing was the yell that would suddenly shatter the dark peace of the evening and then die into an anxious echo. "Watch out, Gebhardt's coming!"

One evening he caught Czuprynski. There and then he merely acknowledged him with cold politeness. "Good evening. See you tomorrow."

But the next day he interrogated him mercilessly and loaded him with extra homework.

Nearby was the female high-school, full of beautiful girls. Like Halina Krolikiewicz, the daughter of the headmaster of the boys' school, and Kazia Zak, who had the most admirers. Some were keen on the theatre. And they already acted at the Sokol, a glorious old gymnastics society, which had become one of the many centres of Wadowice's intense cultural and artistic life.

The two schools had just one theatrical club. And Lolek was the main organiser and actor. He composed verses and directed; his acting was heartfelt, full of tension. He owed a great deal to Mieczyslaw Kotlarczyk, an exquisite writer and artist. But his first "teacher" was Ginka Beer, a Jewish girl with stupendous black eyes and hair, tall, slender and a fine actress. She was two years older than Wojtyla and lived in the same building. She realised at once that the boy was talented.

But Lolek's real triumph was when he played two different roles in *Balladyna*. The boy who was supposed to play Kostryn, the "villain", did not turn up and they did not know what to do. Lolek, who was to appear in the role of Kirkor, the "hero", volunteered to play the second part. He already knew it by heart. So he went on stage without even having rehearsed. And he was a huge success.

CHAPTER FOUR

Jurek had become an assiduous reader of *Nowy Dziennik*, a Cracow Jewish newspaper. As he knew that Gebhardt, a Catholic, did not read it, he would copy out the reports of international politics and present them in class as his own history essays. And, to tell the truth, with excellent results.

But it was from the *Nowy Dziennik* that Jurek began to find out about the wave of anti-semitism that was mounting in central and north-eastern Poland. After the death of Marshal Pilsudski, the "Jews' uncle", as he was called, a government of colonels had taken over. The Parliament was dominated by just one powerful party, the party of national Reunification. And the situation had got progressively worse. Economic boycotting – *Owszem*, as it was called in Polish – had become almost a watchword. And there were many newspapers ready to fan the flames. The *Polska Karta*, playing on its name, adopted this motto: "As fly-paper is to flies, so *Polska Karta* [paper] is to the Jews." Unashamed incitement to hatred.

In Wadowice, the first – as yet muffled – repercussions began to be felt. One day Jurek saw Lolek coming towards him with a sober expression on his face.

"You know that Ginka is going away?"

The girl was studying medicine in Cracow. She had been incriminated for her relations with a friend, whose fiancé was a communist. They went to see her. Her eyes were glistening, it was clear she had been crying, but she knew how to react; her character was strong.

"Have you seen what's happening against the Jews in Germany? Well, something of the sort is going on here too. And I can't take it any more. This atmosphere oppresses me, it's as if I can't breathe. So I've decided to leave. I'm going to Palestine. That's where my land is now."

They accompanied here to the station, but it was she who consoled them. She even managed to laugh. "What long faces you've got! Come on, cheer up. This business will soon by over. Just wait, we'll meet again soon."

One morning – it was already 1938 – Jurek passed in front of his father's study and noticed that the name-plate had been changed. To the name Wilhelm there had been added the Jewish, biblical name, "Zev" (Wolf). It was clearly a discriminatory measure that had been imposed on all Jewish lawyers. He tried to talk about it to his father, but he was evasive, he did not want to create any alarm in the family. He already had enough problems outside the house.

As chairman of the Jewish community, it was his duty to protect the Jews from any discrimination or violence. Moreover, at that very period, Kluger was the handling the case at the Wadowice law-courts against a worker in a paper-mill in Zywiec: this worker, caught stealing, had accused the manager of the factory, a Jew, of having collaborated with the communists during the Bolshevik revolution and having sent numerous Poles to their deaths. The trial was causing a good deal of stir. People were coming from all around to follow it. There was the risk of incidents, even of a pogrom. Fortunately, thanks to incontrovertible evidence given by a Polish general, the worker's claims were shown to be false.

Nonetheless the atmosphere remained tense. At school there were a couple of teachers who resented the Jews. The anti-semitic students had become bolder; they openly declared their membership of the extremist "ND" party. There were continual arguments. Like the day they started to quarrel about the Spanish Civil War and Germany's role. And fists began to fly. The Jewish boys were defended by Czuprynski, Bernas, Kesek, Kus, Wojtyla, Romanski. Always the same ones.

As they stood outside the school-gates they discussed the question. Partly to reassure Jurek, to let him know he had their support.

Kus said: "This is all absurd. The Jews have been

in Poland for centuries, they've contributed to the development of the country. During the Russian occupation they took part in the uprising as well."

Bernas said: "It's not only a question of the past: right now, Poland is taking in thousands of Jews who've been driven out from Germany, by the Nazis."

Romanski put in: "Yes, in Germany there's anti-semitism. Terrible anti-semitism."

And Wojtyla: "Haven't you heard what Canon Prochownik says in his sermons? Anti-semitism is anti-Christian. And when men start to hate their fellow men in this fashion, I fear there are terrible times ahead."

But the worst was yet to come. Jurek and Lolek were on their way home from school when they heard a hubbub in the Rynek. In the square there were groups of insolent-looking youths – all from other parts, there wasn't a single familiar face – with sword-shaped badges in their lapels, the symbol of the NRO, the National Radical Organisation. They were picketing all the Jewish shops, offices and surgeries, to stop the Catholic townspeople using them.

They shouted: "The Jews are part of the worldwide communist plot! Economic boycotting is an act of patriotism!"

But the townspeople were protesting; they refused to accept this outrage. Because of course they knew the owners of these shops, they knew they were good people:

Taffet, the ironmonger, or Balamut, the motorcycle man. And so, thanks to the firm reaction of the townspeople, the disturbance was quickly ended.

But that night the youths returned – or at least, it was presumed that they were the same trouble-makers. They broke the windows of a few shops and houses. Nothing tragic. But the entire town took it as an insult.

The next morning, Gebhardt came into the classroom for the history lesson with a grim look on his face. He explained a few points quickly. He asked a few desultory questions. But for most of the lesson he remained silent, as if lost in thought. He did not seem like the same person.

The bell rang. The teacher made to go out, but in the doorway he suddenly turned back. His eyes were hard, questioning.

"I hope none of my students are to be numbered among last night's hooligans."

His voice softened slightly.

"I am speaking to you not as a history teacher but as a Pole. What happened has nothing to do with the tradition of our Fatherland."

A pause, then he opened a book with the page already clearly marked.

"In 1848 Adam Mickiewicz prepared a sort of political manifesto, which was intended to inspire the constitution of the future independent Slav States. Among other things he wrote:'. . . in the nation everyone is a citizen.

All citizens are equal before the law and before the administration. To Israel . . .' "

By way of explanation he reiterated the point: "That is, to the Jew . . ."

Another pause. Then he continued to read from Mickiewicz's words.

" 'To the Jew, our elder brother, esteem and help on his path towards eternal welfare, and in all matters equal rights . . .' "

Outside the school, that day, there were many parents. The Captain was there too, waiting for Lolek. He seemed more saddened than worried by what had happened. Jurek greeted him as he passed. And by way of response, he gave him a rough caress.

"How is your father? Please give him my regards. Don't forget, will you?"

Lolek remembered an episode from many years back. As he crossed the Rynek with his father, he had seen a man approach Lawyer Kluger and kiss his hand. It was a poor postman, lame and sickly, whom the whole town held responsible for the continual hayrick fires that summer. The only one who believed in his innocence was Wilhelm Kluger. He had defended him in court for free and had got him off.

"But isn't it only priests whose hands you kiss?" Lolek asked.

His father said: "He wanted to thank him, in his own fashion, for the good he had done him."

CHAPTER FIVE

It was a lovely sweet-scented April. Jurek could not remember ever seeing the countryside flaunting such strong bright colours. He had taken Tesia to play tennis at Stanislaw Banas's villa. It was a sumptuous building in the centre of an agricultural village of several thousand hectares, not far from Wadowice. The field of red earth was flanked by an immense meadow of daisies; and at the far end there rose a barrier of acacias, as if to protect it from the wind that blew from the Beskidy mountains.

Tesia was playing against Wiktor Kesek's eldest brother. She looked like a small white elf. Stanislaw, Wiktor and Tadeusz Czuprynski gazed at her admiringly from the side of the court.

"Your sister's got great legs!"

"Jurek, she'll beat you soon!"

Jurek said: "To tell the truth, I think she already can."

Their laughter made Tesia miss the ball.

But it was clear that Wiktor was not his usual self. He gave brusque answers, he was on edge. Then, as if he could no longer contain himself, he addressed his friends seriously. "Have you read Antoni Slonimski's latest book?"

From their questioning looks, he realised at once that they had not read it. "It's a satirical book. Fantastic in a way, a little political, but ultimately frightening. There's a dictator, Retlich, who orders his army to raze Warsaw to the ground. Only two people are left alive, a boy and a half-lunatic, then the Lapps turn up . . . But it's not the story that struck me. What struck me was the madness of that man. Retlich, do you get it? It's more or less an anagram of Hitler."

"Pure fantasy," said Stanislaw.

Wiktor went on: "Fantasy? Look at Austria. What was the Anschluss in actual fact? An entire people handed themselves over to the Reich . . . And suppose the same thing were to happen here, how would Poland react?"

It was perhaps the approach of evening, but it was as if the countryside had suddenly been drained of colour.

Jurek returned home with a sense of anguish. He saw life in his town running along in the same old fashion, serenely, calmly; but at the same time he felt that something unforeseeable was about to happen. And as the days went by, he grew more and more convinced that it would be something tremendous, a major upheaval.

To drive these thoughts away, he buried himself in his studies. A few weeks later he was to take his school-leaving exam. He had to choose which written tests he would do: if he passed them, he would not have to face an oral test in those subjects. He decided on physics, as he felt reasonably on top of it, and history, in which he had a name for himself with Professor Gebhardt, who was also a friend of his father's. But which classical subject? He chose Latin instead of Greek, but with some trepidation.

At the beginning of May Wadowice was host to an important visitor. The Archbishop of Cracow came, Adam Stefan Sapieha. He carried out the confirmations at the parish church. Then he went to the boys' high-school. And, on behalf of the students, Lolek made a speech of welcome.

At the end, struck by the boy's eloquence, Sapieha spoke to the religion teacher. "What does this student intend to do after his exams?"

The teacher said that he had not made up his mind yet.

Lolek, who was just a few feet away, stepped forwards. "Your Excellency, may I tell you?"

"Of course."

"I'm going to enrol in the Polish faculty of the Jagellonic University to study philosophy."

"A pity, a pity," murmured the Archbishop, continuing to gaze curiously at Wojtyla. And afterwards, over lunch with the teacher, he returned to the subject.

"A pity he doesn't want to study theology."

The day of the exam arrived at last. As the room

filled up, Jurek had a sudden inspiration. He saw Lolek choosing his desk and, elbowing his way, he took the seat behind him. He knew that Wojtyla was not the sort to pass notes or to whisper information. In eight years of school he had never done it; maybe out of modesty, not wishing to show that he knew he was the best in the class, or more simply from a kind of natural reluctance to commit even so common a misdemeanour.

Jurek, therefore, did not ask any questions. But when he found himself in difficulties, he began to stare at Lolek's back desperately, as if hoping that he would somehow feel his request for help. He called his name as well, but maybe not loudly enough. However, at a certain point, Lolek slowly moved to one side, leaving his translation in full view. And Jurek was able to copy out the main passages. At the end he thanked his friend with some emotion. And Lolek's only answer was a slightly ironic smile.

At the Kluger house nobody expected him to do so well. When the results came out it was a surprise for everybody. Of course nobody was surprised to hear Lolek's results: he got top marks, *bardzo dobrze*. He had taken written exams in Latin, Greek and Polish and an oral exam in German.

There was a ball. Every year, for the students, both boys and girls, who had passed their school-leaving exams, they organised the "Komers" at the civil servants' club, the most elegant place in town, where the upper middle classes met. All three *salons* were opened up and decorated for the occasion. A well-known local band played for them: Polish songs and dances, like the mazurka, and then waltzes, tangos and foxtrots. But for the boys it was a little disappointing at first. They had all attended dance-classes for the occasion, they had pomaded their hair and donned fashionable clothes: white shirts and ties, wide trousers; some were even wearing spats. And yet the girls seemed to snub them, they danced with older friends, young lawyers from the law-court, officers from the XII infantry regiment.

The students stood sullenly around the side of the dance-floor. They knocked back vodka and stuffed themselves with sandwiches. They made a great show of their first cigarettes in public. And, to draw attention to themselves, they bawled out one of the most popular songs of the time, with the words: "Sapphire, Sapphire, my Sapphire, come to my girl." But then Jurek and Czuprynski, the "Don Giovanni", began a counter-attack. They strode across the room, as if about to challenge someone to a duel, and asked two girls if they might dance with them.

The ice was broken. The soldiers and lawyers retired in good order. When the band started to play a slow fox-trot, all the students dashed forwards. Lolek danced with Halina: and some of his companions sniggered, convinced that there was something between them. Banas and Kus danced languidly, holding the other actresses in their arms, Kazia and Zosia. They went on till the early hours. Nobody wanted to stop. It was a wonderful party. But for many of them it was a moment of parting. They would all take different paths. There was no knowing when they would see one another again.

Jurek and Lolek met for the last time in autumn 1938, in Wadowice. Jurek had gone to Warsaw to follow an engineering course. But he stayed only a month; there was a new outbreak of anti-semitism in the city. At the university the Jews were beaten up, they were not allowed to take seats on the right side of the classrooms. The Klugers decided to send their son to work in a textile factory, hoping to send him as soon as possible to study in Nottingham, England.

In the summer Lolek had moved with his father to Cracow. He had started to attend the university. And he too had witnessed anti-semitic demonstrations; on one occasion he had had to intervene to protect a female Jewish colleague.

Jurek said: "I hear you were a big hit with your poems at the Catholic House." His friend interrupted him brusquely. "Forget about that! Tell me about yourself. What happened to you in Warsaw? Is it true they've really got it in for Jews?"

It was a short fleeting encounter. They were both in a hurry. Or more probably, neither of them wished to say out loud the fears he felt.

"See you soon."

"Yes, sure, I'll come and look you up in Cracow."
"My regards to your family."
"And mine to the Captain."
"Bye, Jurek."
"Bye, Lolek."

CHAPTER SIX

Tesia appeared, panting and with fear written on her face.

"Jurek, Jurek, Daddy wants you to come straight home."

At first her brother didn't understand. That morning he had met up in the park in Wadowice with his Jewish friends, Poldek, Zygmunt and Leopold. They were talking about events in Europe. Just a few days earlier the Ribbentrop-Molotov Pact had been announced.

"They want to split Poland up between them again," said Poldek.

Leopold said: "They've got tanks, cannons, planes. What have we got?"

Zygmunt pulled out all his pride. "Us? We know how to fight!"

Tesia repeated in exasperation: "Jurek, you've got to come!" and turned to leave.

"What's up?"

They could only just hear the girl's words as she ran off.

"War! War's broken out!"

It was September 1st, 1939.

In Cracow, in the Cathedral of Wawel, Lolek was serving Mass for Father Figlewicz, his first religious teacher. Suddenly they heard the sirens. Almost at the very same moment, bombs went off loudly and then there was the stutter of anti-aircraft guns. It was a short, hurried Mass, partly from fear and partly from the wish to go and see what was happening. On the other side of the Vistula German fighter-planes were dive-bombing the suburbs.

Lolek shouted: "My father's at home alone!" and he was off at a run.

Acrid smoke rolled over the streets, many buildings were in flames. There was a final attack, a final clutch of bombs dropped on the radio-station, then the planes disappeared. Lolek ran all the way in anguish. He reached the Debniki quarter and tore into Tyniecka Street, where the Wojtylas were living in a basement flat.

Jurek found his father sitting next to the radio. And behind him, his mother was holding Tesia tight in her arms. The speaker was announcing the last details of the Nazi invasion and the declaration of war.

"The German government has proclaimed the annexation of Danzig to the Reich."

And after a pause, as if his voice had cracked under

the announcement: "All men with mobilisation cards must make their way eastwards and present themselves to their units."

As the lawyer stood up he saw his son staring incredulously at the radio-set.

"Jurek, there's no time to waste. We must leave! As soon as possible!"

He was a military judge. He had to join his unit which had already been transferred from Cracow to Rzeszow, in the eastern region. And Jurek had been called up as well.

"Papa, Papa, are you here?"

His father, his face ashen, appeared at the door.

"Where were you Lolek? I was looking for you, I couldn't find you."

"Papa, we must go, we must escape. The Germans won't take long to get to Cracow."

"But where can we go?"

"I don't know. But let's get away. Then we'll see. Everybody I met was saying to go eastwards. And not to take the train, the German planes are firing on them."

Lolek pulled an old suitcase down from a wardrobe. He hurriedly thrust in a pair of trousers, a coat, a jumper, a few things to eat from the kitchen.

"Come along, Papa."

But his father was staring in dismay at those two bare rooms, as if he were about to leave a palace.

*   *   *

The farewells were heart-rending. Grandmother Huppert, now almost blind, had insisted on rising from her armchair. She stood in silence, immobile. Jurek's mother clung to her husband's hands, as if to prevent him from leaving. And then Tesia threw her arms around Jurek's neck. The women wept. The men, in an attempt to reassure them, could find nothing to say but banalities.

"It's best like this," the lawyer repeated, perhaps in an effort to convince himself primarily. "You mustn't worry about us. As soon as we can, we'll let you know where we are."

As the car drove off, they turned to look back at the women. Only then did Jurek manage to give vent to his feelings. "I feel bad about leaving them all alone like that."

"There was nothing else we could do. Anyway, you'll see, the Nazis won't touch them. They're animals, but they won't dare to hurt the women."

The suitcase was half-empty, but now it was beginning to weigh on him terribly. Because with his other hand Lolek had to support his father. He could see he was tired, still dazed by what had happened. They left Cracow and walked along the road towards Tarnow.

There were hosts of other people with them. Above all Jews. They had loaded cars and carts with impossible burdens. There were mothers pushing babies in prams. Old people being helped along by their grandchildren.

Peasants dragging their cow with them. And from the turmoil there rose a hubbub of songs, prayers, imprecations and sobs. They were driven by the strength that is born of despair. With no goal, no destination ahead of them.

A military lorry passed, forcing its way through the flowing human tide, and Lolek called out: "Please, can you take him with you?"

They pulled his father up and sat him among the ammunition boxes.

Mr. Kluger and Jurek on their way through Cracow, met some relatives. They decided to get into their car and drive eastwards all together. At Tarnow they found a group of soldiers. They had no idea where the division headquarters was. The army had been routed.

"It's all over. They're holding out only at Westerplatte."

The Klugers decided it was better to go on then, towards Rzeszow. There was no water to be had along the road. The wells were empty. There was no bread to be found. And the sun was beating down with the force of midsummer.

They heard the roar of Stukas, far off but getting closer. People dived under the trees and into the bushes. The women protected their children with their bodies. The vehicles tried to zig-zag. But the planes passed back and forth, flying low and firing on everything and everybody: people, animals, cars. And leaving a wake of death and grief behind them.

"Come on, Papa, they've gone."

Lolek helped his father to climb back up the slope. They had rushed down it the moment they heard the echo of the machine-guns' "tatatatatata". The road was practically cut in two by bombs. Everywhere there were corpses, wounded people groaning. Animals running madly through the fields. Nobody knew whether to go on or stay put. Old Wojtyla had no strength left in him. He had walked all the way from Rzeszow.

In the distance they saw a river.

"It's the San!"

"That means we've travelled almost two hundred kilometres!"

From the other side some ragged, unkempt soldiers approached.

"The Soviet Union has declared war on Poland. And the Russian soldiers have already crossed the border, they're advancing. You'd do better to go back to Cracow, even with the Germans there. At least you'll have a roof over your heads."

Lolek looked at his father to give him fresh heart.

"Papa, do you feel up to it?"

"Just let me rest a bit."

*   *   *

After the River San there were fewer people on the road. The car could go faster. Jurek still couldn't believe he was alive, after that hail of bullets just inches away. He saw a child in a meadow. He could not have been more than two years old. He was sobbing and looking around himself in bewilderment. Next to him lay two bodies, probably his parents.

They stopped at Tarnopol. The army was there, but the town was in utter chaos. On September 17th, without firing a shot, the Russians arrived. The local communists were out in the street to welcome them.

"Long live our liberators!"

But the Russian soldiers were like scarecrows. They were clad in threadbare overcoats and had rifles slung round their necks on bits of string.

The Klugers and their relatives decided to turn back, to Lwow. It was a large town, they could probably find some shelter there. What Jurek did not expect was to meet his Jewish friends from school, Zygmunt and Leopold. They went to greet the lawyer. But he looked serious, worried.

"Boys, we must be very careful."

After annexing the eastern zone, the Soviets had started to deport the Poles, in hundreds of thousands, towards the East.

"There's a risk of being sent to Russia or Asia."

Jurek said: "So why don't we escape to Romania?"

* * *

After Cracow, the Germans had reached Wadowice. They drove slowly into the Rynek with a long line of motor vehicles, as if to make it clear to everybody that they were in command now. Rozalia and Tesia Kluger peeped out of the window and watched as they occupied the square and the town. They were frightened. Very frightened.

A few weeks later the Nazis blew up the synagogue.

CHAPTER SEVEN

It was certainly more than forty degrees below zero.

Jurek could no longer feel his hands. His body was more or less protected by his old coat, even though it was full of patches. But his feet, which sank into the snow, were frozen. And his hands – it was as if they had been lopped off. He couldn't even hold his axe any more. Two of his companions collapsed on the ground, exhausted. But the Russian soldiers prodded them with their bayonets and summoned them harshly back to their duties. "Get on with it! You've got to cut down ten more trees today. Otherwise you won't go back."

Jurek thought he would die, as he gazed at the immense forest of Siberian pines they were supposed to fell.

He and his father had been there for five months. In June 1940, some soldiers had burst into their room in Lwow and dragged them onto a train. The same fate had befallen their relatives and their friends. Jurek saw Zygmunt and Leopold for the last time as they were forced on board another carriage. But he was unable to speak to them. There was an enormous crowd. Two million Poles were deported to the Soviet Union around that time.

The journey was gruelling. Seventeen days that seemed like years. Without even knowing where they were being taken. Then they arrived in Maryjskaja, in the north of Russia. A "re-education camp" it was called. In actual fact it was a concentration camp. It consisted of a cluster of wooden huts, which were poor protection against the biting cold.

The guards had had a minimum of respect for the oldest men – many were in pitiful shape – and had given them less strenuous tasks to carry out. Lawyer Kluger, for instance, had been given a job as warden. But the younger men spent all day outside, even in the blizzards, cutting down trees. At night they were exhausted. Even if they were ill, they were given no respite. There was no doctor. There were no medicines. And as for food, for the rest of his life Jurek was unable to shake off a sensation of unappeased hunger.

One day, on his way back to the camp, he was in really bad shape. He kept striking his legs with his fists, to get the circulation going; but it was as if they belonged to someone else. He took heart only when he saw his father greet him with a smile and beckon him. He followed him into the hut; they went into a corner, lit the last stump of candle, and the lawyer drew out a letter exultantly. It was from home, from the women.

The Klugers, on their arrival in Maryjskaja, had at once dashed off a few lines with their address and entrusted it to the Red Cross. And now, incredibly, an answer had come.

Tesia began, with her rapid, nervous handwriting. "Dearest Papa, dearest Jurek, how are you?" There was then something crossed out, probably by the German censors. ". . . Life has become difficult, but they haven't persecuted us. Mama and I have been put to work in a paper-mill . . ." A few more lines crossed out.

They were followed by Rozalia's rounded, elegant handwriting. "Don't worry about us. And don't torture yourself for having left us in Wadowice. You were right to do so. My mother couldn't move, her eyesight gets worse and worse . . . You are in our hearts. This storm will soon pass. And let us hope to meet up again, all together, at home."

As Jurek read, his tears smeared the ink, magnifying his mother's words: ". . . at home."

But the letter did not and could not tell the whole truth. In Wadowice, Wiktor Kesek had been killed by the Germans. His two brothers had been shot as well. Zbigniew Silkowski had been interned in a prison camp near Magdeburg. And as for other school-friends . . .

It was snowing in Cracow, but Lolek still wore his wooden clogs. The dark-red overalls hung loose about him and hampered him at his work. He broke the blocks of travertine; then he dragged the barrow full of stones down from the quarry to the railway where they would be loaded onto the trains. Every so often, the worker whose job it was to set the tube of explosive into the rock would ask him to lend a hand.

Lolek had been obliged to look for a job, to get hold of a good "work card", an *Arbeitskarte*. If he were found without one he would have his ration card withdrawn and get sent off to Germany. So some friends had found him this job at the quarry of Zakrzowek, which was owned by the Solvay firm. A companion from the university worked there, Juliusz Kydrynski.

Juliusz and he no longer went to the "Alma Mater Jagellonica". It had been closed. Shortly after the Wojtylas returned to Cracow, there had been a sudden round-up. All the most prominent professors had fallen into a trap and been arrested; they were locked up in the concentration camp of Sachsenhausen, where many of them later died.

For Lolek it had been a shock to see the stupendous city under the Nazi yoke. To see the flag with the black swastika fluttering on the Sandomierz rampart of Wawel Castle, where the governor general Hans Frank had taken up residence. And the swaggering attitude of the Germans when they entered the shops specially reserved for them – *Nur für Deutsche* – where they could buy everything, meat, white bread, vegetables, butter. While the Poles had to queue up at four in the morning, with the temperature 20-25 degrees below zero, just to buy a miserable ration of black bread.

Lolek's spirit had been wounded by all this. But when his own teachers were arrested, including old Nitsch, with whom he had just taken an exam in contemporary Polish, he had a deep personal sense of the barbarous treatment that was being inflicted on his country.

In those days he often called on his friend Juliusz at his family home. And he would also visit the Szkockis' villa on the River Vistula, where they held evenings of theatre, music and poetry. It was only in private houses, and always with extreme caution, that it was now possible to engage in cultural activities of any sort. The last important theatrical performance had been Nizynski's play, *The Cavalier of the Moon*, three months before the war broke out; Lolek had played a part in it as well. After occupying the country, the Nazis closed the theatres, forbidding all cultural enterprises.

Grandmother Szkocka was the moving spirit behind these artistic evenings. And she took young Wojtyla to her heart. She urged him to join the "Unia", a clandestine movement which, among the various forms of resistance to the Nazis, attributed great importance to artistic commitment, in particular to the theatre.

On entering the organisation Lolek swore an oath. He vowed to fight with the "weapon" of language and to defend the national identity, that Poland might regain her freedom. In the words of Mickiewicz's poem, the *Pan Tadeusz*: "... It is war, war for Poland, brothers, we must fight!" But as Norwid intended it: "I persevere in the idea that insurrection with the sword must be accompanied by insurrection of thought".

One morning Lolek was out walking with his father. A group of Jews passed, recognisable by their armbands with the star of David. Two German soldiers were prodding them along with their pointed rifles and insulting them by repeating the words on the signs that hung outside certain shops: "Entrance forbidden to Jews and dogs".

Old Wojtyla watched them sadly. "Where are they taking them?"

"I don't know, Papa. They say the Nazis are going to create a ghetto here, like the one in Warsaw. There are also rumours that they're going to be deported."

Lolek wrote to Kotlarczyk, who was still in Wadowice. He expressed his solidarity to his friend, who had had two brothers arrested. But he also reflected bitterly on Poland. He ended: "I believe that our freedom must be the door of Christ ..."

Was he thinking of his country or also of himself, his own life?

CHAPTER EIGHT

The silence of Maryjskaja was suddenly shattered by a shout. But it was a shout of joy.

"We're free! Free!"

One of the deportees had heard the news and run to tell the others.

In June 1941 Hitler had declared war on the Soviet Union. Poland's government in exile had stipulated an agreement with Stalin, by which the Poles could enrol into the Polish Army to be formed in Russia.

One after the other, the prisoners stumbled sleepily from their huts. At first they didn't understand, they couldn't understand. But then, like a ripple of ever-widening circles, the news spread from mouth to mouth. Jurek and his father embraced, tears running down their faces. Everyone seemed to have gone mad. Finally they lit a bonfire in the middle of the camp, under the impassive eyes of the Soviet guards. And some of them started dancing around the flames.

The problems arose the next day. Nobody knew where the Polish army was. So the Klugers set off blindly. They thought that it was anyway best to make southwards. They managed to get onto the train which till then had been used to carry the timber away from Maryjskaja. They got as far as the city of Joskar-Ola, near Kazan, then the Volga. And the river was at least a definite point of reference.

They boarded a large boat crammed almost to sinking point. There was not a square inch of free space, and they had to keep their eyes open if they didn't want to get robbed of everything. Some people had not eaten for days; the effects of the war were really beginning to tell. There were families of German origin who were being transported to Asia. There were young men evading military service. And there were hosts of ex-deportees, people with nowhere to go, wandering from one camp to another.

The boat stopped briefly at Kujbysev, and only at the very last moment did the Klugers notice that there were Polish military police on the bank. They disembarked and enlisted immediately. Everybody was welcome, the army was still being formed. It was not discovered till afterwards that thousands of Poles had been prevented from leaving Russia and had thus been forced to fight alongside the Soviets.

Lawyer Kluger was put in charge of one of the recruiting stations. Jurek, after passing the admission exam, was transferred to Kara-su, in the Fergana valley, to attend the artillery officers' school.

His mind was in turmoil when he boarded the train that was to take him thousands of miles away, to the slopes of the Himalayas. It was the first time in his life he had ever been alone. He gazed at his father on the station platform, noticing how old he suddenly seemed to have become, and as he said goodbye he found it hard to smile.

The Captain seemed to be resting, but he was lying in a strange position: half his body was out of the bed. He had not been well since Christmas. He found it hard to carry out the housework. The Wojtylas' house in Tyniecka Street, in Cracow, was small; it was not difficult to keep tidy. But he felt overcome by weariness; even just preparing a meal or mending a pair of shoes exhausted him. He no longer went out to the literary evenings with Lolek and his friends. He preferred to stay at home, lying on the bed. Like that February 18th.

His son had gone out to get his medicine from the surgery. On his way back he had called in at the Kydrynskis'. His friend's mother, as on other occasions, had prepared lunch for him. And Maria, Juliusz's sister, had come back with him to help heat the dishes up.

"Papa, it's me. I've got the medicine. Maria's here too."

Lolek called out to let his father know he was back.

He went into his father's room and saw him in that strange position. He tried to lift him but felt that his hands were icy-cold. He let out a cry and Maria came running from the kitchen. The girl bent down to listen to the old man's heart, realised that it was all over and turned to her friend with a gentle expression.

Lolek, without letting go of this father's hands, knelt down. He was crying. He could not forgive himself for not having been there. It had been just the same when his mother died, and then when his brother died.

"Just like the other times," he moaned, "why wasn't I with him? He was all alone."

He stayed there all night, next to his father's body. And he realised that he was now on his own. Entirely on his own. He was not yet twenty-one.

His life changed from that moment. It was then perhaps that the conviction grew on him that he had to follow another path, that his was a different vocation. He continued to work at the quarry. He kept up his artistic and literary commitments. Indeed, now that his house was empty, he put up Mieczyslaw Kotlarczyk, who had managed to make his way to Cracow with his family. And, together with some other colleagues, they founded the Rhapsodic Theatre, the famous "theatre of the word".

But Lolek confided his inner torments to a new friend, Jan Tyranowski. A rather strange sort. Forty years old, though he didn't look it. Fair hair and blue eyes, a shy, rather old-fashioned air about him, but great charisma all the same. He had trained as an accountant but worked as a tailor. And he devoted all his free time to apostolic work among the youth of the parish of St Stanislao Kostka, in the Debniki quarter.

"I just can't forget that day, when Papa died," Lolek said. "I keep praying, almost stubbornly, but I just can't forget it."

Tyranowski said: "I understand your sorrow. What I can't understand is how you can pray without feeling that your father is close to you."

"Maybe it's a question of the way I pray."

"There are different ways of praying, of course. But one fundamental sort of prayer is the mystical, contemplative sort, which goes to the very depths of your soul. I may not be the right person to explain it to you. Try and read St John of the Cross, St Teresa of Avila."

"All right, I'll try."

"And why don't you take a group of the Living Rosary? You know how to talk to other people, the boys listen to you."

"But wouldn't they take more notice of a priest?"

"Not always. And anyway, haven't you heard? Some of the priests here in Debniki have been arrested. They may even have been deported."

"To a concentration camp?"

"Nobody knows. But they say that the Nazis are doing terrible things to the Jews."

"They say, they say! How is it nobody ever knows anything for certain?"

In the Klugers' house in Zatorska Street, Wadowice, the Gestapo had set up their headquarters. One day a German officer had simply turned up with two soldiers and requisitioned the flat.

"By tomorrow you must be out of here!"

Rozalia, Tesia and her grandmother had thus moved to a little house in one of the working-class parts of town. Rozalia's brother, the lawyer Bronislaw Huppert, and his wife and daughter, Wanda, had come with them for the same reason.

They all did what they could. The lawyer started up a primary school and taught the children himself. His wife and daughter set up a kitchen to feed the poor.

Tesia helped the Hupperts. She was kept busy all day. At night she studied. But within herself she felt increasingly perturbed. It was true she was with her mother, her uncle and her aunt. But now that her father and Jurek were gone, now that her home, her "shelter", was no longer there, she felt lonely, terribly lonely. Lonely and defenceless.

CHAPTER NINE

"Do you know what they call this place?" Jurek asked.

The girl shook her head.

"The valley of Fergana, according to the legend, was where the earthly paradise lay . . ."

But the girl did not seem to understand.

"Don't you remember? Where Adam and Eve lived . . . the story of the apple, the snake . . ."

Still no sign of understanding. Maybe, Jurek said to himself, she doesn't know the religious story; there's been atheism in Russia for years; or maybe she's being sly, she's just pretending not to understand. He thus decided to go straight to the point. "What I mean is, this is a place that encourages love-making."

The girl burst out laughing. She had understood perfectly well, she had just been leading him on.

"Couldn't you say so quite simply, without all that beating around the bush?"

Jurek was bewildered.

The girl went on: "Look, if I come with you, it's

not just to get away from the front. If I ever should decide that I don't want to go to war, I'll find another way . . ." and she took his hand.

Against the dark background of the Himalayas and under the starry canopy of the sky, Mascya was even more beautiful. She was eighteen years old. She had fair hair, a slim, supple body with firm calves; you could tell she was a dancer. She was one of the 300 pupils of the Bolshoi who had turned up unexpectedly at Kara-su a few days ago.

In the ex-tuberculosis sanatorium, alongside the artillery course, they had set up one for nurses. The Bolshoi students were only the first young women to arrive: the students, for some reason, were all from dance-schools or artistic ensembles. A welcome surprise for the hundreds of Soviet and Polish soldiers. All the more so since the girls had just one expedient they could rely on to avoid being sent to the front line: to get pregnant. And even at this distance, the war terrified them.

"So you weren't pretending to love me just to . . ."

"No, silly boy," Mascya said.

They were walking hand in hand, with the thrilling scents and sounds of a tropical evening around them, but they were sad. In another week or so Jurek would have to leave. He had finished his courses in artillery and astronomic topography. He was to join the Polish army, which, after General Anders' quarrel with Stalin, had been allowed to leave Russia for Persia.

And so, with thirty or so compatriots, Jurek left the earthly paradise. He went by train to Krasnovodsk, boarded the ship which was to take him to the other shore of the Caspian Sea, to Pahlevi.

At Krasnovodsk, to everyone's surprise, fifteen or so girls from the Bolshoi (although Mascya was not one of them) got off the train as well. With perfect nonchalance they walked through two long lines of guards from the Soviet political police, passed through the road-block declaring themselves "Poles", and then calmly boarded the ship. Nobody could work out how they had managed to get away from Kara-su.

The journey was not over for Jurek at Pahlevi, however. An opium-dazed lorry-driver took him to Habanija. From there he travelled by bomber to Egypt, "on loan" to the English VIII army for the battle of El Alamein.

"Do you want some more bread?"

That day too, the canteen-girl went out of her way to visit the water-purification department. It was clear that she was by no means indifferent to the young man working there. And everybody had noticed.

He was kind, he put on a smile for her.

"No thanks, I've got enough," he said and he went back to his mess-tin.

Lolek had been moved from the stone-quarry to the Solvay factory, back in Cracow. His job consisted of transporting wooden pails, hanging from a bar, which contained a hydroxide solution of calcium, and sacks of phosphorus and sodium. When he heard the midday siren, he would kneel and pray. But nobody made any comment. He was a dutiful, responsible worker. And besides he often did the others a favour by choosing the night-shift.

In the winter he would sit by the boiler heater. And he would pull out the books Tyranowski had given him, like the *Dark Night* of St John of the Cross.

"I had no other light or guide/Than that which burned in my heart./This was the light that led me/More surely than the midday glare . . ."

Lolek read the Spanish mystic, and his mind went back to his conversations with Tyranowski. Thanks to him, he had learnt a new approach to the faith.

"He wanted," he would later recall, "our souls to rediscover the religious truths, but not through a filter of prohibitions and restrictions; he wanted us to draw upon those supernatural founts which, as he believed, we are born with, and derive from them a model of human existence lived in the supernatural, spiritual dimension . . ."

He had now made his mind up. The theatre was no longer enough. He wanted to become a priest. One October day in 1942, still dressed in his factory over-alls, he went to Archbishop Sapieha to tell him of his decision. And he began clandestine courses at the faculty of theology.

It was more difficult to tell his theatre colleagues. He did so at the end of a rehearsal, thinking that he might be able to conclude the argument more quickly in this way. Instead they talked all night. They all tried to dissuade him – Kotlarczyk, Tadeusz Kudlinski, Halina, and other friends.

Kotlarczyk seemed to think he wanted to become a monk.

"Do you think you can solve everything by shutting yourself up in a monastery?"

Kudlinski even fell back on Norwid, one of Lolek's favourite authors. "Do you remember what he wrote in the *Promethidion*? 'Light does not exist to be kept under a bushel.' And Norwid took it from a passage in St Luke's Gospel!"

But it was all to no avail: Wojtyla remained firm.

"You see, at a certain point in a man's life, his destiny is fulfilled. After long following the light that glimmered in my darkness, in the dark night of my faith, I have now found my vocation, my mission."

For a while, Lolek kept up his theatrical activities. Always in secret, in private houses. One evening there was a moment of panic, when a loud, imperious announcement was made from a loudspeaker in the street.

"The Wehrmacht high command announce that the German armed forces have reached the western bank of the Volga. Stalingrad is expected to fall within days."

It was just propaganda. But it was all part of the Nazi

regime's strategy: to spread the myth of its invincibility and thus strike its enemy psychologically as well, spreading fear, maintaining a constant climate of menace.

The following day, Lolek heard that Juliusz Kydrynski had been deported to a concentration camp.

Wanda took Tesia to one side.

"Tonight Tadek is taking me away."

The suburb where the Klugers and the Hupperts were living in Wadowice had been turned into a Jewish ghetto. It was fenced round and guarded night and day by German soldiers.

Some people, with help from outside paid for with money or jewellery, had managed to escape to the mountains. This idea had been proposed to Rozalia and Tesia as well. But they had refused. They were afraid they might not make it, and anyway it would mean leaving their grandmother. Old and blind as she was, she could not possibly take part in such a venture.

"It's best that we all stick together, they won't touch us," Rozalia had said.

But Wanda could not bear it any longer, she wanted to get away. Her fiancé, Tadek, had promised to come. When darkness fell, the young man approached the wire-netting, managed to slide underneath, and cautiously made his way to within a few yards of Wanda's house. Behind the window she was waiting to jump out and run away.

But suddenly a shot flashed out in the darkness. And then came a cry. Tadek must have been hit. Wanda ran out screaming but her father rushed after her and pulled her back in.

Silence once again, a grim silence. And a thin trail of blood. Which continued beyond the wire-netting.

CHAPTER TEN

Jurek could not believe his eyes. He was in Iraq, in the desert near Kirkuk. And one day, like ghosts, his old school-mates appeared before him: Czuprynski the "Don Giovanni", Romanski, Kogler the "Marshal" and Bernas. For four years they had heard nothing at all from one another. They embraced emotionally. They spent the night in a tent drinking and recounting their various stories, how they had escaped from Poland and how they had joined Anders' army.

Jurek waited for a long time, he did not have the courage to ask. Finally, almost against his own will, he got the words out.

"Any news from Wadowice?"

They all said that they had been away for ages. No, they knew nothing. But Czuprynski said it without looking Jurek in the face. And Jurek noticed.

"Please. If you know anything, tell me."

Tadeusz spoke thickly. "It seems they've created a Jewish ghetto in Wadowice. But I'm not sure about it."

Jurek closed his eyes and clenched his fists in an attempt to expel that image.

Lolek was on the night-shift at the Solvay factory. He was walking along the side of the road, in Konopnicka Street, when a military vehicle struck him from behind, knocking him into a ditch. The driver did not even realise and drove straight on. But a woman had seen what happened. She made a car stop and they took the unconscious young man to the hospital. Wojtyla came round eighteen hours later; the wound in his head healed quickly, but the doctors prescribed a long convalescence. He went to spend it at the Szkockis' house.

"A period of spiritual retreat," he told himself, "contrived by God."

He studied, prayed, spent whole days in meditation. He became more convinced than ever that he had made the right decision.

One afternoon Grandmother Szkocka entered his room without knocking. She was red in the face. She was almost stuttering.

"The Nazis have destroyed the Jewish quarter in Warsaw! And it seems they want to wipe out all the ghettos in Poland."

Lolek felt a shiver run up his spine. He thought of his own city, his Jewish friends, their families. He closed the book in front of him, and started to recite the Our Father.

*　*　*

It was very hot in Wadowice, that July in 1943. But Rozalia had closed the windows all the same. She felt safer like that. Or at least it was one way of warding off the evil that lurked outside. Tesia tried to stir a little breeze around her grandmother with a postcard.

Suddenly they heard footsteps. Rough, heavy steps. A violent crash at the door, which gave way at once. Four Germans charged in, one after another. The women could not even speak. They waited, motionless, frightened.

The first man to enter spoke in a low cold voice: "We must take her away!" and pointed at Grandmother Huppert with his rifle.

Rozalia stood in front of him. "No! You can't do this!"

The Nazi turned the gun on her. "Orders, orders from above! Old people and children are to be taken to the concentration camp."

"But it's cruel! She's old! She's blind!"

"There'll be someone to look after her."

Two other Nazis pulled Grandmother Huppert to her feet and started to drag her out. Tesia, who had clung onto her grandmother, was hurled to the ground brutally. Rozalia had no idea what to do.

"Murderers! Murderers! You'll kill her like that!"

The one in command snapped the safety-catch of the gun and pointed it at Tesia.

Rozalia froze, then her arms dropped helplessly to her side. And she pleaded: "At least tell me where you're taking her . . ."

"To Belzec."

The fourth German murmured, as he left: "And nobody returns from Belzec."

But the women did not hear him. And anyway the name meant nothing to them as yet.

A few weeks went by, and the Nazis returned. But this time there were hundreds of them. They ran with Alsatians on leads through the narrow streets of the ghetto, forcing their way into all the houses. When they came out, they were driving terrorised men and women in front of them.

Rozalia carried herself upright, with dignified pride: it was as if she had already foreseen everything that was happening and was indifferent to it. Tesia was wearing a fine dress, almost out of defiance, but every so often she reached out for her mother's hand. The Hupperts were there too. There were many other friends and acquaintances, lined up along the street.

They reached Targowica Square, where the cattle market was held every Thursday, and Rozalia caught a distant glimpse of their house in Zatorska Street. The Nazis had built a rough stockade all around so that no-one could escape. The crowd of prisoners swelled. More Jews arrived under escort from all the nearby villages. There were certainly over a thousand of them. They looked around themselves fearfully, not talking or moving. Even those who were crying did so in silence, stifling the sobs.

An SS officer entered the enclosure and approached a man dressed in black who was clutching a violin-case to his breast. He seized him by the arm and dragged him out of the crowd.

"Play! Play something! But something cheerful, get it?"

The violinist hesitated, looked around himself in a daze, as if seeking sympathy. The officer resolved his doubts by pointing a pistol at his temple.

"I told you to play!"

But the man had just started when the people started shouting: "Stop it! Stop it! That's enough!"

He started to open the case to put the instrument away, but a soldier struck him on the back of the neck with his rifle-butt, knocking him to the ground. Blood was flowing from the violinist's face and hand. He pulled himself to his feet, took hold of the bow and started to play again. A shrill, almost heart-rending note sounded. It was the officer who stopped him this time.

"Stop it, bastard."

From the other side of the square a man in civilian clothes squeezed his way through the crowd. There was no need for him to ask. He passed and the prisoners handed him money and precious objects, necklaces, bracelets, earrings. A woman stared at him with blazing eyes. "Filthy traitor! You're a Jew like us. Aren't you ashamed?"

And she pulled out some banknotes, tore them up and hurled them into the extortioner's face.

A soldier struck her several times with his gun, and the woman collapsed to the ground in a pool of blood.

The loudspeaker made the final announcements. "You will now make your way in an orderly fashion to the station. You will then set out for a work-camp where you will find food and shelter . . ."

The column marched sadly off.

An old woman approached the Hupperts. "Wanda, your Tadek is alive. He's wounded but alive. He's sent word that you're not to worry. He'll wait for you."

Wanda did not know how to express her joy. She looked around for Tesia but could not see her.

Tesia was weeping silently as she walked alongside her mother. Rozalia put her arm around her shoulders. Her daughter looked at her, and she found the strength to smile again. A tender, gentle smile. Then Rozalia put her lips to Tesia's forehead, and Tesia clung to her mother.

They climbed into the railway-carriage still hugging one another. The iron door closed with a sharp metallic sound.

On the door, outside, there was a single chalked word: Auschwitz.

CHAPTER ELEVEN

Early in the morning Jurek climbed to the top of Mount Cairo. He and the other map-readers had to co-ordinate the artillery, deploying a force of more than one thousand two hundred guns. They worked rapidly, preparing things for the battle of Montecassino.

It was a decisive battle, but it started badly. The first offensive, on May 11th, 1944, failed. Quarrels broke out among the officers. Some were furious. They claimed that General Anders had blundered badly.

"It was suicidal," they said, "to send the soldiers out without any cover. The Germans were well-sheltered in their bunkers among the rocks. It would have been better to go round the mountain and attack from the rear."

But a week later, these criticisms were already forgotten: Montecassino was finally taken. Romanski, who had been wounded three times, and Bernas were awarded the highest decoration for military valour.

After Montecassino, it was the turn of Rome. And then the Adriatic front. They proceeded from Osimo to

Ancona, where Czuprynski died. Poor Tadeusz never spotted the mine, his body was ripped apart by the terrible explosion. Jurek, who was in the front line, was told about it and went straight back, but he could not even pay homage to his friend's body. There was no time for sentiment in war. The VIII army advanced from Ancona to Cesena. And then up the Via Emilia to Forli and Faenza, under the continual attack of the German guns.

Jurek had two hair-breadth escapes. The first was at Piedimonte Alta, when the tank he was travelling in was shelled: fortunately, they were able to open the hatch underneath; there were no rocks or stones and they managed to dig a hole and stay untill night fell, when they escaped. And one foggy evening at Brisighella, after imprudently going out to play poker he found himself behind the enemy lines and then, minutes later, in a minefield.

That August 7th – "Black Sunday" – Lolek escaped capture by pure chance. The German soldiers were combing the city inch by inch. Their orders were to round up all the men and take them to concentration camps.

The previous week the Warsaw uprising had broken out, the population had taken up arms in support of the partisans. But the Nazis had managed to get the upper hand. Partly because the Red Army, situated on the other side of the Vistula, had obeyed shameful orders from Stalin to stay where they were and just look on.

And so, to prevent the same situation from arising in Cracow, the Governor General had decreed a massive round-up. The soldiers searched the house in Tyniecka Street as well, but did not go down into the cellar, thinking it was uninhabited. Lolek was in fact at home, standing behind the door, his heart pounding.

A little while later, a priest came to fetch him; he had been sent by Sapieha to take him to the Archbishop's Palace in Franciszkanska. Sapieha had decided to get all the clandestine seminarians into safe-hiding. As soon as Wojtyla arrived, he put on a cassock: if the Germans came, he would pass for an acolyte.

The journey across Cracow, with the Nazis patrolling the streets, was a dramatic one. Lolek made it, however, and breathed a sigh of relief. But he was immediately given a tragic piece of news. A friend of his, Andrzej Zachuta, had been shot. They had discovered that he was working for the organisation that assisted the Jews.

In the early months of 1945 Anders' army launched a new offensive on the River Senio. Bologna was liberated on April 21st. Kluger's platoon halted at Castelbolognese. And it was there, one afternoon, that Jurek was summoned by Captain David Kupferman, a distant relative.

The Captain was kind — too kind. What could he be after? He invited him to sit down, offered him a

77

cigarette, but would not come to the point. Jurek was puzzled.

"What's the matter, David?"

Kupferman avoided his eyes. "Bad news, Jurek."

"From my family? From Wadowice?"

Kupferman skirted round the subject. "You know that my job often entails being in contact with the security services and the Red Cross. I was looking for my fiancée. She had been interned in Bergen Belsen . . ."

Jurek stood up and interrupted him. "Look, David, are you going to tell me what's happened?"

The Captain's voice was barely audible. "Killed."

"My mother, my grandmother?"

Kupferman lowered his head in a slow affirmative gesture.

Jurek let out a shout: "No!" Then he clutched onto the edge of the table, as if to give himself strength.

He asked in a pleading tone: "And Tesia, my sister?"

This time the Captain was unable to reply, even with a nod.

But there was no need. Jurek understood. In his heart the last thread of hope snapped. He dropped onto a chair, holding his head in his hands and sobbing: "Poor Tesia . . . My poor family . . ."

There were huge explosions now almost in continuation. The Germans were leaving Cracow, blowing up the bridges over the Vistula behind them. An even larger

– or closer – explosion shattered the windows on the first floor of the Archbishop's Palace.

Lolek was down in the cellar, together with Sapieha, the priests, and the other seminarians. The Archbishop was leading them in reciting the Rosary. They all responded devoutly, but many of their voices were trembling. Lolek prayed with his eyes closed, so as not to be infected by the general atmosphere of fear.

Towards dawn the explosions ceased. There was another long, agonising wait, while the light of the new day filtered down to the cellar. It was now truly over. The Nazis had gone. For ever. The priests and seminarians emerged. There was a festive air in the streets. Meanwhile the first Soviet tanks and military cars rumbled into the city.

Lolek ran as fast as he could to the Debniki quarter. He wanted to see his friends. A few days later Zbigniew Silkowski came to see him; he had just been set free from his prison camp. He had heard of the Captain's death, but did not know that Lolek had decided to become a priest.

Life was returning to Poland, but there were many missing faces. And often nobody knew what had become of them.

After the war Jurek stayed for two years in Italy. He took up his engineering studies again at the Polytechnic in Turin. He had no wish to return to Poland. He did not want to return to places that would remind him of his family, his mother, Tesia. And he did not want to return to a Poland that was now in the hands of the communists. Particularly because the Polish communists – as everyone said – were a mere front for the Soviet Union, for Stalin. Which meant that the Nazi tyranny was being replaced by another tyranny; the fact that they were at opposite political poles counted for nothing.

In 1947 Jurek was demobilised in England. His father was there. He got a degree at Nottingham Technical College. He told himself that he would put down new roots in that country. He married and had two daughters. The climate of Leeds, where he had found work, proved deleterious to the health of the younger daughter. And so, in 1954, they moved to Italy, to Rome. Jurek started up a small firm with Kurt Rosenberg, a friend from childhood days.

It seemed a temporary solution. But it turned out to be definitive. Wadowice, Poland, the war, Auschwitz, were a story that could not be cancelled. But Kluger preserved them in the most intimate, private corner of his memory.

The date was November 2nd, 1946, and the place, the crypt of St Leonard in the Cathedral of Wawel, in Cracow. Kotlarczyk was there. Halina was there. And so were almost all his colleagues from the Rhapsodic Theatre. Grandmother Szkocka, Father Figlewizc and some friends who had come specially from Wadowice were there too. But not Tyranowski, even though he had been so instrumental in bringing about the occasion. The tailor from the Debniki quarter had just died and thus never saw Wojtyla celebrate his first Mass. Cardinal Sapieha had decided to bring forward his ordination to the priesthood so that he could go to Rome to complete his studies.

"There is a difficult period ahead of us," he had told him, "and the Polish church needs well-prepared priests."

The day before his departure, Lolek met Jan Kus. Jan was about to enter a sanatorium to be treated for the tuberculosis he had contracted in the underground army, called AK.

"And the others?" Lolek asked.

Jan just said that some school-friends had fought in the Italian campaign, some in Tobruk, others in the RAF or in Poland, in the ranks of the national army.

"And where are they?"

Jan did not know.

The fate of so many friends seemed shrouded in darkness. The war was over in military terms, but only now were people beginning to understand what it had really cost.

CHAPTER TWELVE

Jurek read one file after another. His desk, in his little office, was covered in paper. Matters were urgent. He was endeavouring to secure an important deal, with several million lire at stake. He started to dash off an answering letter. What was the date? Ah yes. He had just written it – Rome, November 20th, 1965 – when Kurt Rosenberg interrupted him.

"Listen here," and he read him an item from the paper. " 'Yesterday, at the Ecumenical Council, the Archbishop of Cracow, Karol Wojtyla, made a speech . . .' Does that name mean anything to you?"

Jurek was about to make a sharp rejoinder; he wanted to get on with his work. But then the name caught his attention; he raised his eyes from the letter. He thought about it for a moment. Then he shook his head. "No, it's not possible. He wasn't a priest. I don't know what became of him."

"You never heard from him again?"

"Nothing. I feel as if I left Poland centuries ago."

"But there was a Wojtyla, a Karol Wojtyla, in your class. The one who acted."

Jurek started to picture him. "Lolek, that's what I called him, Lolek. There was something special about him. The first in the class, in the theatre, the first in everything. If he had gone to General Motors, he would have become chairman . . ."

"And couldn't he have become Archbishop of Cracow instead?"

"Well, now you mention it, yes. He was very religious."

Jurek got up, started walking around the office. He stopped in front of the book-case, then the map of Poland. Suddenly he turned to Kurt.

"Hang on!" I've just remembered something definite. It was the day we took our school-leaving photo. Wojtyla was on the right. He had a strange ironic look about him. But he always had that ironic look."

"And so?" said Kurt.

Jurek made up his mind at that point. "You know what? I'll have a go."

He returned to the desk, picked up the phone-book, flipped through it. "Here we are, Polish Institute, Via Pietro Cavallini. It must be somewhere near Piazza Cavour. He could be staying there."

He dialled the number. "Hello, I'd like to speak to Archbishop Karol Wojtyla . . . He's not there? Ah, he's not back yet . . . When he gets back, could you please tell him that Jerzy Kluger called, yes, Kluger from Wadowice. My number is 856200 . . . Thank you."

He put the phone down as if he had lifted a great weight from his shoulders. "Better that way. Better not to have found him in. If it is him and he wants to get in touch with me, he'll know what to do."

He started walking around the little room again. He was on edge. He sat down, arranged his papers, then stood up again. When the phone rang, he snatched it up. But his voice was timid as he said: "Hello? . . ."

At the other end, a strong, clear voice: "Who's speaking? Is it Jerzy Kluger, the Kluger I know?"

Jurek said even more timidly: "Yes, it's me. So I wasn't. wrong . . ."

The voice at the other end, in a confidential tone, said: "Jurek, come over straightaway. I'll be expecting you!"

A frenetic drive through the traffic-clogged streets of Rome, and forty minutes later Jurek was entering the Polish Institute. A young priest led him into the waiting-room.

"His Excellency will be along immediately."

Jurek heard a door open behind him, turned and found himself facing Karol Wojtyla. He had not seen him for twenty-seven years. He had changed very little: his hair was grey, but the face was the same as ever. They smiled at each other, but did not speak. The Archbishop opened his arms wide, they embraced.

"Jurek, you haven't changed."

"Neither have you, Your Excellency."

"What do you mean, Excellency? Call me Lolek, as you used to."

Jurek murmured the name that took him back to his childhood days, to his youth.

"Lolek, yes, Lolek . . ."

He was moved. He couldn't speak.

Wojtyla rescued him. "Shall we go for a walk?"

They left the Institute. They walked side by side. Every so often they looked at each other, with both curiosity and surprise. Evening was drawing on. And as darkness descended, so they grew more confidential. They made their way towards Lungotevere Prati, then to San Pietro.

Wojtyla asked him: "Where have you been all these years?"

Their faces were serious, almost hard, as they talked of people who had died. Jurek's tale was a long, uninterrupted tragedy.

". . . Zygmunt and Leopold, do you remember? Selinger and Zweig were with me at Lwow. They were deported to Russia too. Then they were freed, they were making their way by boat along a Siberian river, the boat capsized, they drowned . . ."

"Poor Leopold, poor Zygmunt! And did you hear about Wiktor, Wiktor Kesek? The Nazis shot him in Wadowice."

"War . . . Just think. I saw Tadeusz Czuprynski at

Nettuno, after the liberation of Rome. And a month later he died in the battle of Ancona."

Wojtyla covered his eyes with his hand, to hide his emotion.

"Poor Tadeusz! He was so in love with life! But your mother, Jurek. And Tesia ... How terrible. Truly terrible."

Then he asked: "And what about your father, Lawyer Kluger?"

"He died three years ago. After the war he lived in London."

In Piazza San Pietro they stopped and gazed at the basilica. Then they made their way back to the Institute. At the door, before saying goodbye, Wojtyla made a promise to his friend. "Whenever I come to Rome, I'll get in touch."

"Promise?"

"Promise. And then we can both go and see Zdzislaw, Zdzislaw Bernas."

He read the amazement on Kluger's face.

"After the war Zdzislaw stayed here. He married an Italian, he's a dentist in Eboli."

"Fine, next time you're here, we'll go and see him."

"I can't tell you what a surprise it is to see you!"

"For me too. After the battle of Montecassino, I lost touch with everyone."

"In the meantime, Jurek, I'd like to help you get back in touch with your old school-friends. You know, in

1958 we celebrated the twentieth anniversary of our school-leaving exams in Wadowice. We did it in our old classroom, the one on the second floor."

"I'd love to see them again!"

"Well, why don't you? Is it always going to have to be me coming here? Or will you make it back to Poland one day?"

"No, for the moment I don't feel up to it. Just remembering is hard enough. Seeing things too – no! It would be too painful!"

They both held their hands out to shake them. But then they embraced. As Wojtyla gazed into his eyes, he said something that surprised his friend. Or at least something he was not expecting. "One day, all Jews and Christians will be able to meet in this fashion."

Kluger did not know what to say. He just said: "Let's hope so. Anyway, thank you."

Then with a smile: "Bye, Lolek."

"Bye, Jurek."

AUTHORS NOTE

I met Jerzy Kluger in 1977, by chance, in Rome. I had just returned from Poland, where I had been carrying out an investigation for my newspaper, and he asked me if I had met his "school-mate", Karol Wojtyla. A year later the Archbishop of Cracow was elected Pope. I at once sought out Kluger for an interview. But he had some doubts. "What are people going to think of a Jew who claims to be a friend of the head of the Catholic Church? . . ."

Eventually, after a good deal of insistence on my part, he agreed. He talked to me about Wojtyla's youth, their friendship in Wadowice in the thirties, their friends at high-school, the fun they had. But Kluger also told me about his own life, the terrible fate of his mother, his sister and his grandmother in the Nazi extermination camps. And I have to confess that I was taken aback by the apparent coldness with which he recounted his family drama.

We agreed that I would show him the interview before publishing it. We met in Piazza del Popolo. It was pouring with rain. Kluger stepped out of his car, climbed into mine and started to read the text. He suggested a couple of corrections. When he reached the point in which I had written about his family, he suddenly changed. He started to look through the sheets quickly, nervously. He gave them back to me without finishing them. He got out of the car and stood for five minutes in the pouring rain. But not even the rain could hide his tears.

I pondered over it for some time. And my conclusion was always the same; it was the only possible one. For the first time in over thirty years, Jerzy Kluger had been forced, by reading those pages, to relive the tragedy that had struck his family; he had been constrained to tear it from the depths of his memory. Where he had confined it not out of a desire to forget – definitely not that – but from a need to survive.

It was thus that I understood what the Holocaust had really meant and what is continues to mean today. Not just a genocide, an unprecedented crime, perpetrated against a whole nation. Not just the martyrdom that had been inflicted on the Jewish people, with their 6,000,000 victims. But also the deep, unhealable wound that had been gouged for ever into the flesh and into the conscience of those who survived. Those who, despite all, are called upon to remember and to bear witness.

I decided that one day I would write this story, as it had been told to me. It is essentially the story of friendship, of a relationship which strikes one by its very "normality". A friendship that sprung up in the classroom, grew stronger through the years of their boyhood, was dramatically interrupted by the war – where the two young men lived through adventures that, although entirely different, were somehow parallel – and then resurfaced after the conflict and continued even after Karol Wojtyla's election to the Papacy.

At the same time, it is the story of a friendship that takes on a symbolic resonance in the context of the Church's change of attitude, sanctioned by Vatican Council II, towards the Jewish people. The Catholic friend is the first Pope after 2,000 years to enter a synagogue, the synagogue of Rome. There, in front of his Jewish friend, also present in the temple, he repeated the Council's condemnation of all forms of anti-semitism and addressed the Jews as "elder brothers".

We can also recall John Paul II's words at Oswiecim (Auschwitz): "As Pope I could not fail to come here." In affirming his Polish origins, he claimed that he had thus been able "in a certain sense" to share the Jewish people's tragedy. This new attitude of the Church must be read in the light of Wojtyla's personal history, and in particular of that of his youth.

In June 1991, in Warsaw, he said to the representatives of the Polish Jewish community: "A man lives events on the basis of his own experiences. I belong to that generation for whom co-habitation with the

Jews, the Israelites, was a fact of everyday life." In the following August, at Wadowice, addressing his old school-companions, he recalled the "special letter" that he had consigned to "one of our companions" (i.e. Jerzy Kluger) to be read out at the inauguration of the plaque on the site of the synagogue.

This letter was of course the starting point for the account of this singular friendship. In telling the tale, some necessary liberties have been taken in reconstructing scenes and conversations that took place fifty or even sixty years ago. But the essential truth of the story has been respected throughout, and it is this truth and its message which the book most wishes to impart, particularly to the young. With an earnest solicitation that they should not only learn the tragic history of the past, but also do all they can to ensure that the future – the history we are living right now – repudiates for ever the temptations of racism, discrimination, hatred, and contempt for man. For any man.

APPENDIX
*Unabridged text, in English translation, of the letter
sent by John Paul II to Jerzy Kluger*

Dear Jurek,

On the 9th of May of this year, 1989, on the site of the
Synagogue which was destroyed during the last World War,
a plate will be unveiled commemorating the Jews from Wadowice and near-by, who were victims of persecution and were
exterminated by the nazis.

I thank you very much for the letter in which you advise
me of this event. Many of those who perished, your co-religionists and our fellow-countrymen, were our colleagues in our
Elementary School and, later, in the High School where we
graduated together, fifty years ago. All were citizens of Wadowice, the Town to which both you and I are bound together
by our memories of childhood and youth.

I remember very clearly the Wadowice Synagogue, which
was near to our High School. I have in front of my eyes the numerous worshippers, who during their Holidays passed on their
way to pray there.

If you are able to be there, in Wadowice, on the 9th of May, tell all who are gathered there, that, together with them, how I venerate the memory of their so cruelly killed co-religionists and compatriots and also this place of worship, which the invaders destroyed.

I embrace with deep reverence all those whom you are remembering this day – the 9th of May 1989 in Wadowice.

Allow me to quote the words, which I have pronounced to the representatives of the Jewish community of Warsaw during my third pilgrimage to the Fatherland:

" The Church and all peoples and nations within this Church are united with you ... Indeed, when they speak with

warning to people, nations and even to the whole humanity, they place in the forefront your Nation, its suffering, its persecutions, its extermination. Also the Pope raises His voice of warning in Your name. This has a special significance to the Pope from Poland, because together with You, He survived all that happened in this land". (14th June 1987).

Should you consider it proper, you can read this letter in public.

I greet you from my heart

Vatican, 30th day of March 1989

Jan Pawel II pp.

Mr. Jerzy Kluger
via F. Denza 19
00197 Roma

Drogi Jurku,

W dniu 9 maja br. na terenie synagogi zburzonej
w czasie ostatniej wojny zostanie odsłonięta tablica
dla uczczenia pamięci Żydów z Wadowic i okolicy, którzy stali się ofiarą prześladowania i zostali zgładze-
ni przez nazistów.

Bardzo Ci dziękuję za list, w którym mnie o tym
powiadamiasz. Wielu z tych zgładzonych Twoich Rodaków
i Współwyznawców było naszymi kolegami w szkole podsta-
wowej, a później w wadowickim gimnazjum, w którym wspólnie zdawaliśmy maturę przed pięćdziesięciu laty. Wszyscy
zaś jako Wadowiczanie byli obywatelami tego Miasta, z którym obaj - zarówno Ty jak i ja - jesteśmy związani pamię-
cią naszego dzieciństwa i młodości.

Synagogę wadowicką dobrze pamiętam, znajdowała się
w pobliżu naszego gimnazjum. W oczach mam jeszcze szere-
gi wyznawców, którzy w dniu świątecznym udawali się do
synagogi na modlitwę.

W.Pan
Inż.Jerzy KLUGER
via F.Denza 19
00197 Roma

Jeśli udasz się na dzień 9 maja do Wadowic, powiedz Tym, którzy tam się zgromadzą, że wspólnie z Nimi wspominam Ich pomordowanych Rodaków i Współwyznawców oraz to miejsce modlitwy, które zostało zniszczone przez najeźdźców. Otaczam głęboką czcią to wszystko i tych wszystkich, których pamięć w dniu 9 maja br. pragniecie uczcić w Wadowicach.

Pozwól, że na koniec przytoczę jeszcze słowa, jakie wypowiedziałem podczas spotkania z przedstawicielami wspólnoty żydowskiej w Warszawie w czasie mojej trzeciej pielgrzymki do Ojczyzny:

"Kościół, a w tym Kościele wszystkie ludy i narody czują się z Wami zjednoczeni ... Owszem, wysuwają niejako na pierwszy plan Wasz naród, jego cierpienie, jego wyniszczenie, wtedy, kiedy pragną przemawiać do ludzi, do narodów i do ludzkości głosem przestrogi; w imię Wasze podnosi ten głos przestrogi również Papież. A Papież z Polski ma do tego stosunek szczególny, ponieważ razem z Wami jakoś przeżył to wszystko tu, na tej ziemi" (14 czerwca 1987 r.).

Jeśli uznasz za stosowne, możesz ten list publicznie odczytać.

Serdecznie Cię pozdrawiam

Watykan, dnia 30 marca 1989 r.

Jan Paweł II pp